Time for Writing
in the Elementary Sch

Clearinghouse on Reading and Communication Skills
1111 Kenyon Road, Urbana, Illinois 61801

National Council of Teachers of English
1111 Kenyon Road, Urbana, Illinois

THEORY &
RESEARCH
INTO
PRACTICE

Time for Writing
in the Elementary School

Eileen Tway
Miami University, Oxford, Ohio

Published 1984 by the ERIC Clearinghouse on Reading and Communication Skills and the National Council of Teachers of English, 1111 Kenyon Road, Urbana, Illinois 61801.

This publication was prepared with funding from the National Institute of Education, U.S. Department of Education, under contract no. 400-83-0025. Contractors undertaking such projects under government sponsorship are encouraged to express freely their judgment in professional and technical matters. Prior to publication, the manuscript was submitted to the Editorial Board of the National Council of Teachers of English for critical review and determination of professional competence. This publication has met such standards. Points of view or opinions, however, do not necessarily represent the official view or opinions of either the National Council of Teachers of English or the National Institute of Education.

Contents

Foreword

The Educational Resources Information Center (ERIC) is a national information system developed by the U.S. Office of Education and now sponsored by the National Institute of Education (NIE). ERIC provides ready access to descriptions of exemplary programs, research and development reports, and related information useful in developing effective educational programs.

Through its network of specialized centers or clearinghouses, each of which is responsible for a particular educational area, ERIC acquires, evaluates, abstracts, and indexes current information and lists that information in its reference publications.

The ERIC system has already made available—through the ERIC Document Reproduction Service—a considerable body of data, including all federally funded research reports since 1956. However, if the findings of educational research are to be used by teachers, much of the data must be translated into an essentially different context. Rather than resting at the point of making research reports easily accessible, NIE has directed the ERIC clearinghouses to commission authorities in various fields to write information analysis papers.

As with all federal educational information efforts, ERIC has as a primary goal bridging the gap between educational theory and classroom practice. One method of achieving that goal is the development by the ERIC Clearinghouse on Reading and Communication Skills (ERIC/RCS) of a series of booklets designed to meet concrete educational needs. Each booklet provides teachers with a review of the best educational theory and research on a limited topic, followed by descriptions of classroom activities that will assist teachers in putting that theory into practice.

The idea is not unique. Several educational journals and many commercial textbooks offer similar aids. The ERIC/RCS booklets are, however, noteworthy in their sharp focus on educational needs and their pairing of sound academic theory with tested classroom practice. And they have been developed in response to the increasing number of requests from teachers to provide this kind of service.

Topics for these booklets are recommended by the ERIC/RCS National Advisory Board. Suggestions for topics are welcomed by the Board and should be directed to the Clearinghouse.

Charles Suhor
Director, ERIC/RCS

1 Theory and Research

Writing is more than the act of transcribing meaning-bearing sounds to graphic symbols on paper. What happens on paper is only a small part of the process; it is only the outward manifestation of a complex thought activity. The whole process of writing cannot be confined to set periods of time in a school day, and, for this reason, school class periods are not conducive to any but the most perfunctory kinds of writing. For more inspired writing, instruction must break away from assignments that require neat, prescribed pieces to be turned out at a given time and turn toward providing opportunities for young writers to gather ideas, live with the growing ideas, put them on paper, get reader response, revise, polish, and share beyond the classroom. Since school days continue to be compartmentalized into rather rigid time segments, it is often a problem for teachers to provide the kind of time necessary for all that is involved in writing, from "off-stage rehearsal" (the term used by Donald Graves [1982] to describe writing that occurs off page) to final copy.

To find out more about what happens when children write in school, I took cues from the work of Donald Graves (1975) and Janet Emig (1971), and conducted longitudinal observations of the writing processes of middle school age children. The observation design called for sitting with the children in the classroom, keeping running records of observations and interviews, and keeping samples of the children's writing in a case-study type of approach to learning more about what happens in children's writing.

Three students, one each in sixth, seventh, and eighth grades, agreed to participate in the project and were the main participants throughout, although many more students were at times involved. (The study was conducted at the McGuffey Laboratory School, Miami University, Oxford, Ohio.) Elizabeth, sixth grade; Mike, seventh grade; and Jim, eighth grade; all entered into the project, knowing that it was an effort to find out and understand more about what happens during the writing process. The students were patient and thoughtful in the face of probing questions and participated in interviews throughout the school year (and the following one) with unflagging cooperation.

Early in the project, I asked Elizabeth if she wrote a lot on her own, outside of school.

"Oh, yes," she said. "I usually have a story a day in my head, but I don't write it down because that might make me forget it."

I was surprised that writing down could lead to forgetting, since usually one writes things to keep or to remember, and I asked about this. Elizabeth explained that if she wrote her story down, it would stay that way and she might forget the *whole* story, but in her head she could continue to add to it and change it. "Maybe someday," she said, "I will write it all down."

Further conversation with Elizabeth about her writing revealed that she *did* write in her school notebook at home. I asked her if the stories in her head were better than the ones in her notebook.

"Just different," she responded. "Much different." She continued, "At school they require a page, and I write a page, but, you know, most of the ideas are in my head. I tried to write down some of the stories in my head, but it didn't look as good as it is in my head. I keep adding things. It would probably take one hundred pages to write it down. For the time being, it's better in my head, so I keep it there."

Elizabeth's words are a good reminder that the process is fluid while the product is fixed, and that there is much to be done with the process in order to improve the product.

Elizabeth says, "They require a page, and I write a page."

Researcher Donald M. Murray says that when we understand the process better, "many articulate, verbal, glib students who are over-rewarded for first-draft writing may be released from the prison of praise and high grades and encouraged to write much better than they ever have before" (1978, 100).

To encourage the Elizabeths in school classrooms to do their best writing, we do need to release them from "writing-on-demand" constraints.

Phillip Lopate, poet and author, reports, "It always amazes me, after I have taught a creative writing lesson and handed out paper, that the children write any poems at all. I could never write a poem in such a vulnerable, exposed situation. Yet they do write often fine poems, at gunpoint as it were" (1978, 141).

However, Lopate goes on to say that serious creative writing requires withdrawal: "Writing is a long seclusion" (1978, 142). He says further that waiting is half the discipline of writing. Elizabeth seems already to know this about waiting and writing. But where is the waiting time in school? One day in frustration, Elizabeth said, "I feel very loaded down at the moment. How am I supposed to write with all of this going on: playing two instruments, Junior Great Books, and assignments?"

Yet Elizabeth likes to write and thinks that her best stories are in her head. She will write them someday because she wants to write. In the meantime, she writes on assignment. These assignments are not likely to represent Elizabeth at her best. Donald Graves' research shows that children write best on unassigned topics (1973).

In the seventh grade, Elizabeth still faced the same time constraints that she did in the sixth grade. In response to a question about her writing at school, she said, "To tell the truth, *that* isn't the only writing I do. I always have stories going in my head. I *am* writing, but I just don't have much time to put it down on paper."

Other students reported similar needs for time to write. Mike, in the eighth grade in the second year of the study, was writing a murder mystery inspired by a visit to a family that lived in a big, mysterious-looking house. "How soon after your visit to the family did you start to write the story?" I asked.

"In about a week," Mike responded. "I'd sort of been thinking of the story all week and planning it out in my mind."

"So you think about an idea for awhile before you ever put pen to paper?" I asked to confirm what he was saying.

"Yes. You get an idea and you sort of go with it. A lot of times ideas come to you in the strangest places. When I'm going to sleep, or I first wake up, are the two times when I get my most inspirations. Or sometimes I will see something or read something that I want to put in it [the story] somehow—and work that in."

"This story is one that you're doing on your own, not a school assignment?" I asked.

"Right, although I may put it in my journal."

At the time of our discussion, Mike had been working on the story for one week since he had started putting the story on paper, and he had completed two pages. It had been two weeks since he got the idea for the story. Mike confirmed that a lot of the writing was going on outside the paper. He said, "A lot of ideas are tentative. There are a lot of different branches that I may take, but a lot of it, I haven't decided on yet. A lot of it is just so abstract."

He explained "abstract" by saying, "I haven't really got the ideas down to a fine point yet. I've got a lot of ideas that are just floating around that I haven't really elaborated on yet."

When one thinks of two weeks of thinking and two pages of writing, one realizes that this kind of process can be a major problem for teachers trying to fit writing into regular school periods. We need to continue to study the phenomenon of time and writing, but there are practices that lead to bringing abstractions to the reality of written products. Some classroom-tested activities will be suggested in the Practice section.

The Uses of Memory

> There seem to be two significant forms of memory employed by the writer: one is the way in which writing unlocks information stored in the brain; the other is the memory of what the writer has previously written within the piece, which influences each choice during the process.
>
> Donald M. Murray (1978, 95)

For some students, indeed for most that I have observed, it is the immediate memory, or the more recent memories, that trigger writing ideas. (Note the previous discussion of Mike's response to a visit to a mysterious house.) Once the initial idea is harbored and is allowed to take its place in memory, then "older" memories, memories of life experiences all along the way since the writer has had conscious memory, come into play. Thus, both older and newer memories are resources for the writer, and may intertwine. Then, according to Murray, the immediate or more recent memories of what has been written to develop the idea so far also come into use. It would be tedious to have to look back over pages endlessly as one writes; some things must be kept in memory. However, a writer needs to look back from time to time to ensure accuracy and continuity.

To help us understand what does actually happen in writing, we need to observe the process carefully. George H. Henry suggests that such observing gives us "views of the English classroom as it flows *through time*" (1980, 4). We begin to see that not all writing time is spent in putting words on paper. Looking back over one's composition, for example, takes time from the actual writing down of ongoing ideas, to say nothing of all the other distractions that may occur in any given writing session.

In one forty-five minute language arts period, I observed Mike (seventh grade) in the process of writing a page in his notebook. Mike was well into his page before I took the chair next to his. First, I observed him from a distance. My own observation diary reveals the following writing behavior:

> There—in the middle of the classroom, Mike is writing away in a notebook. A paperback sits on the desk beside him. He pauses, contemplates a moment, then gets back to his writing. Now he looks up, probes absently inside his mouth, in his cheek, with a finger, exchanges a casual remark with a classmate, and gets back to his writing, clutching his short pencil and moving it deliberately through the intricacies of English letters. He seems intent, or is it intense?
>
> His head is held low over his work. It is almost on top of the short pencil. The book on his desk is *Ceremony of Innocence* by

James Forman (Dell, 1970). As I move in to see the book, Mike looks up almost imperceptibly, then goes on writing. I sit down in the seat next to him, but as the student occupant of my seat returns, I have to move and this causes Mike to look up. Now he is talking with someone in the row in front of him. Mike goes back to work for a few seconds. Then the teacher, Mrs. D., talks to a student in an adjacent seat, and Mike looks up, then back to his writing. Now, hardly a minute later, a boy in front of him is showing Mike his final copy of the book he is working on. Mike then gets up on an errand.

Soon Mike is back, writes one line, and then *looks back through his notebook*.

"I have to try reading the story; I have forgotten everything that I put down," he says to the student in front of him. He gives a helpless little laugh and continues poring over previous pages in his notebook. Now he is looking off into the distance, chin in hand.

The boy in the front row, adjacent to him, begins to talk to Mike. Mrs. D. moves in to confer with the other boy about his work, and Mike goes back to writing intently as though he had never stopped. This lasts for about one more line. Then he *leafs back through his story*. Now he leans back in his seat, legs crossed, foot swinging, and stares off into space.

Next Mrs. D. is sharing with everyone some comments about the kind of pen to use on final copies of their book projects. Mrs. D. is mid-classroom, close to Mike. Mike attends to her. Then he goes back to writing, maybe another half line, before looking off again, chin in hand.

Mrs. D. says clearly to another student, "Good, Peter! Wonderful, good, fantastic."

Mike looks up.

Then Mrs. D. calls for William, who is writing so intently that he doesn't hear. Mike and others take up the call, "William!"

"Now that's someone who is busy, working. He's writing so well that he doesn't hear," Mrs. D. observes.

Mike writes two or three more sentences in the last few minutes of class. Mrs. D. gives final directions for the class, as the period winds to a close. Altogether, Mike has written about one page in the class period.

As class ends, I ask Mike to finish the sentence, "I like writing when . . . ."

Mike says, "I like writing when I don't seem to hear anything else, when I'm concentrating on my writing."

Classrooms do not seem conducive to the kind of concentration desired by Mike, but it *can* happen, and did for William, at least, during this particular period. Mike's classroom is relatively quiet with carpet on the floor; it is goal-oriented; and the students are cooperative. Yet, even so, there are inevitable distractions, from the teacher, from other students, from others who enter the classroom: messengers, parents, university personnel, etc. In addition, the student seems to make some of his own distractions in this case: by talking, by staring off into space, by leafing back through his notebook, and so on. One must consider, however, whether these moments are really distractions or necessary components of the writing process. The talking had to do with the writing at hand, as nearly as I could tell.

At one point the boy in front of Mike wrote a note to Mike in the form of a mock review, supposedly from *The New York Times,* "An exquisite piece of writing that captures the young reader's mind." The boys laughed about it, but their humor was probably important in relieving tension and it may have reflected their enjoyment and satisfaction in the shared writing experience. The staring off into space may well have been a time of reflection, of decision making, and of searching the memory. Mike said he was reading the story again because, "I have forgotten everything that I put down."

The implications are strong that time must be allowed for stopping, for reflecting, for rereading what has been written, *during* the writing process. Memory needs prodding, stimulating, refreshing, and the writer should not have to wait until the product is completed to take time to reread.

Janet Emig says that "a unique form of feedback, as well as reinforcement, exists with writing, because information from the *process* is immediately and visibly available as that portion of the *product* already written. The importance for learning of a product in a familiar and available medium for immediate, literal (that is, visual) rescanning and review cannot perhaps be overstated" (1981, 74).

Immediate memory is reinforced by rereading, but memories of details of an observed world may or may not be readily accessible in any given writing time. Moments of reflection seem highly necessary for memory probes. Some children develop memory aids, such as drawing. Jim, eighth grade, drew his way into every story he wrote. He drew cartoon scenes for the complete story; then he wrote it out. When he did nonfiction research for reports, Jim pictured things and events in his head. He said, "Sometimes I keep the way they look in my head and write them."

It may be that some students who write about the same incident or the same kind of story over and over either have barren memories due to lack of experience or have difficulties in retrieving a wide range of memories. Varied real and vicarious experiences, such as literature experiences, should help the student who is on a kind of writing plateau to break out of these bounds and draw upon newer memories. A story like *Ramona Quimby Age 8* by Beverly Cleary (Morrow, 1981) may stimulate writing about one's own family or school life.

Time for rich experiences, time for discussing what these experiences mean to children, time to relate these experiences to previous ones, and time to write about them are musts for a viable writing program. It is also essential that time to write include time for memory probes during the process.

J. C. Birnbaum (1982, 241–60) reports that in a study of selected fourth- and seventh-grade students, the more proficient students paused longer to deliberate over topics, related ideas, and possible organizations to represent their meaning to an audience. Birnbaum found that while the more proficient students were writing, their activities and their patterns of pauses indicated that they continually monitored their evolving texts and evaluated their choices in view of their purposes. Birnbaum reports, however, that the less proficient students seemed to be stringing discrete ideas and words together with little regard for overall meaning or the anticipated needs of the reader. Their thinking tended to be additive rather than evaluative.

The implications are clear that teachers must help children see that writing is more than adding words and ideas together to fulfill an assignment. Certainly, not allowing writers time to pause during the process, or time to take stock of the writing, will weaken the product. As the more proficient writers in the Birnbaum study demonstrated, there must be pauses for evaluative choices and changes, based on a rich store of information: memories, purposes, and audience.

Choices and Changes

In the subsection on The Uses of Memory, I described how Mike took time to reread his writing as he went along. Only he knows *how* he was reading his copy or *how* he was using information gained. He implied he was refreshing his memory when he said he had forgotten what he had written. According to Donald Murray, "Writers perform a special, significant kind of reading when they read their own writing in process." He explains, "They must . . . read with an eye to alternatives in content, form, structure, voice, and language." Finally, Murray asks, "How do they read their own page and visualize the potential choices which may lead to a clarified meaning?" (1978, 95).

Mike was evidently reading past writing to get a perspective on future directions and decisions.

In one of our conversations, Mike compared decision making in writing to decision making in the game, Dungeons and Dragons: "In the game, sometimes it's just totally a random decision. If there are two doors, I just pick one of them at random. At other times there is some basis for the decision. You may have some prior knowledge that will help you." Mike said that in writing you always have to take into consideration what is already in the story as you are making new decisions.

Elizabeth, at about the same time, explained about her own decision making, when after observing her and Mike for awhile, I asked her directiy about it. She answered, "When I come to a part where two different things could happen, I let my mind go blank. Then I imagine what would happen if I chose one way. I follow it through in my mind and see what would happen in the story. If I don't like what happens, then I choose the other thing. And sometimes it just comes to me and I write it down, and it's no big decision."

Once again, there are implications for *time*. Not every decision can be a snap decision, carrying writing right along without interruption. It takes an understanding teacher, one who understands children *and* writing, to be tolerant of a student who lets her mind "go blank" in the middle of the language arts class. Nothing will appear to be happening. Maia Wojciechowska once told of being asked what she was doing when she was a child at school and responding, "Thinking." "Well, stop it," the teacher directed. The event provoked her father into taking her out of that school (Eldridge 1976). As Wojciechowska's father knew, *time to think* is essential to the education of a thinking person.

In fact, dawdling time seems to be a requisite for the thinking writer. Donald M. Murray writes, "Even the most productive writers are expert dawdlers. . . . They sharpen well-pointed pencils and go out to buy more blank paper, rearrange offices, wander through libraries and bookstores, chop wood, walk, drive, make unnecessary calls, nap, daydream, and try not 'consciously' to think about what they are going to write so that they can think subconsciously about it" (1981, 171).

In support of the importance of subconscious thinking, Frank Smith says that writers have little conscious control over the actual flow of words at the moment of writing, just control over whether or not to use what comes. He says finally, "We can make decisions about words when they are manifest, when they are accessible to conscious inspection in the imagination or on paper" (Smith 1982, 106).

Birnbaum, mentioned earlier, reports that more proficient writers reread their writing and planned ahead during pauses in the writing process. These students' later explanations for their pauses included selection of an appropriate word, idea, or structure, and revision of these elements for stylistic reasons. In contrast, less proficient writers in the Birnbaum study seldom reread their writing. They scanned for errors, such as punctuation or spelling mistakes, but engaged in no revision for ideational or stylistic reasons. They tended to write only on assignment and to avoid internal evaluation.

For more or less able writers who have to write on assignment, or to produce on cue, often in a limited period of time, it is obvious that, whatever their ability, they do not have the opportunity to do their best. Birnbaum tells of a fourth grader who had to write a story in a given episode of time and who commented on the story she wrote, "This isn't my story. I would have done it differently if I had enough time" (1982, 256).

For proficient writers everywhere, choices and changes seem to be influenced by anticipated reader needs, what has come before in the writing or what the writing so far mandates, ideational and stylistic standards, enough time to make careful decisions, and writer interests and satisfactions.

Interests and Satisfactions

All the time in the world will not help, of course, if there is nothing to write, nothing to say. For writing to come to life, a writer must be involved, must feel a commitment and *want* to say something. As Wendell Johnson once said, one "can't write writing;" one has to write something (1962). Obviously, there must be satisfactions or purposes if one is to immerse oneself in such a complex and strenuous thinking process as writing entails, and until the mind is engaged with something significant to the writer, any writing done is likely to be perfunctory.

To find out about writing satisfactions, we can begin with ourselves as writers and ask what motivates us to write. We may write to communicate messages, to keep records, to express feelings, or to find out more about what we know or feel about something. These purposes, or motives, are ones, then, that teachers can share with children. Adults cannot take for granted that children understand what writing can do for them. Fluent writers, adult or child, *know*; teachers need to know so that what they are asking children to do will be valid; and children need to know, for otherwise their writing will be an empty exercise.

It is likely that satisfactions are very much the same for all writers, whether they are professional or amateur. Professional writers often say that writing is an act of discovery for them, a way to discover what they want to say. Many talk of writing to "surprise" themselves (Murray 1978, 101–03). Elizabeth, when in seventh grade, wrote, " . . . writing is not just a bunch of sentences written down on a piece of paper, but ideas that combine well to make a story. Writing is a wonderful process." According to Elizabeth, her writing provides entertainment, for herself first, and then perhaps for others.

Mike, in eighth grade, wrote, "When I write, I have total mastery over my environment, and I can change it at my leisure. . . . Ever since I was a little kid, I was mad because I couldn't master things and have them happen the way I wanted them to. In writing and in computer programming, everything happens the way I want it to happen." Mike has discovered the power of writing, or composing.

To discover meaning, entertainment, or power in writing, students must feel a personal involvement in what they are doing. Time for composing, then, also includes time for composing the self, time for putting the writer inside the writing. The activities in the Practice section are designed to "stretch" time and to foster involved, purposeful writing.

2 Practice

Ideas and suggestions for practice that will accommodate both the off-stage and the on-stage process of writing are offered here. The first part will provide suggestions for discovering when the extra writing time is needed and by whom, and the second part will provide ideas for incorporating more off-stage, thinking time into the language arts curriculum.

Identifying a Student's Writing-Time Needs

To find more time for the whole writing process in school, teachers must first know more about the nature of the time needed and what is involved in the process itself. Activities to employ to learn more about the whole writing process include both teacher observations of children's writing behavior (studying on-stage writing) and teacher-pupil writing conferences (learning about off-stage writing).

Teacher Observations of Children's Writing Behavior

Guidelines and Suggestions for Observing

1. Be more aware of the time children actually spend on writing a draft on paper and the proportion of that time to the whole process, which may include pencil sharpening and getting materials ready, false starts, time to mull over ideas, looking back over what has been written, looking up spellings, asking questions of classmates or teacher, and rewriting. Keep running notes of what is happening and learn about *real time* involved in writing. Look at posture and other kinds of body language, and observe the context of the writing experience.

2. Earn the right to "watch." Show interest and care for what the child is doing, not critical or oppressive watchfulness. Make observations as unobtrusive as possible in the child's writing experience. Ask questions in an attitude of respect for the writer and the writer's work. (Donald Graves [1983], author and researcher, says that he receives a child's piece of writing the same way he receives a published author's writing.) Choose the moment and ask questions carefully and sparingly during the writing time, and save most questions for the writing conference.

3. Respect privacy. Be both outsider and insider as the situation seems to warrant. Keep distance when a child is engrossed and apparently writing fluently or when a child seems to need to be "alone." Move in closer, draw up a chair beside the writer, and sit in companionship during the writing, when such a procedure seems comfortable. Observe in long views and close-ups as skillfully as a good photographer does. For most teachers, the long view will have to suffice much of the time, since they are responsible for too many children to participate in great numbers of close-ups. However, a teacher does not always have to observe from afar, or observe the whole class. Teachers can learn a lot by "zooming" in on one child from time to time.

Ideas and Implications for Classroom Practice

1. Establish an "Everybody-Writes Time." A teacher is always an observer, but to free time for a more concentrated observation and for note taking, arrange for a regular "Everybody-Writes Time" in the classroom schedule. This sustained, silent writing time (like its counterpart in reading classes) can run for twenty or thirty minutes on one or two days each week. The teacher's writing time, then, is spent in observing and note taking. To participate as much as possible in the personal experience of writing together, the teacher should also try to do some creative writing from time to time along with the class. This special time for observation and writing should be in addition to teacher observations *whenever* writing is going on in the classroom.

2. Carry a small notebook or clipboard for writing and note taking. When keeping running notes, the observer can write about one particular condition that he or she is looking for at a given time, such as time spent in actually writing on paper, or the observer can write down everything that he or she sees and then discern if there is a pattern emerging. Nothing is irrelevant when keeping running notes.

3. Encourage children to ask the teacher questions about his or her personal writing, too. If teachers are open with children about their own satisfactions and problems with writing, then a feeling of trust is developed. An observer who is open and not afraid to reveal his or her own writing joys, concerns, or problems invites equal openness.

4. Share writing efforts. Observing and writing do not always have to be silent. Sharing and discussing what is happening during writing will help build a sense of the community of writers in the classroom. It takes very little more time to talk about writing *during the process* than it does for the writing itself and seems to help the quality of the project (Beeker 1970; Dyson 1982).

Teacher-Pupil Writing Conferences

Guidelines and Suggestions

1. Think of the conference as a special kind of close-up observation. It is an extension of teacher observations in the classroom.

2. Pull in a chair and talk about what is happening during the writing (on-stage). It is all right to have a preset focus, i.e., some questions that seem appropriate for the situation, but take cues from the child. Capitalize on what is going on at the moment. Be flexible enough to follow a promising lead or cue. In short, be a good listener as well as interviewer.

3. Look for specific things in the writing that bring interesting questions to mind, or talk to the child about questions he or she has about the writing. The conference offers an opportunity for the teacher to learn more about what is happening during the writing process, but it also provides for an exchange of information. It is a time for the teacher to respond to the writing with questions or comments that help the writer.

4. Ask thought-provoking questions, rather than ones likely to elicit "yes" or "no" responses. Both teachers and pupils will learn more from questions that evoke thoughtful answers. The following are possible questions:

> How (or where) did you get the idea for this story?
>
> What do you like best about this story so far?
>
> Have you had any problems with your story?
>
> What helps you most with your writing?
>
> What gets in the way of your writing?
>
> Can you tell how you make decisions when writing?
>
> What is going to happen next in this story? Do you know what's going to happen very far ahead?
>
> What happens when you get to know your characters? Do they ever take over, or seem to "take charge" of the story?
>
> Can you explain this part?
>
> Can you tell more about . . . ?

5. Talk about what happens when the child is not writing, but still getting ideas, planning, or thinking about writing (off-stage writing). The following are possible questions:

> Do you write at home, too?
>
> How do you get ideas?

Do you jot notes when you get an idea? How do you remember all of your ideas?

How long is it after you get an idea for a story or other kind of writing until you start writing—actually putting words on paper?

Are there more stories going on in your head than you can write?

What's not yet on paper that you would like to write down?

Do you listen to yourself telling the story in your head?

Do you have to stop sometimes and think about your ideas some more before you can write again?

What do you do during these stopping times? Do you read over what you have written so far?

Do you have to stop sometimes and just get away from your writing for awhile?

6. Share purposes. Let students know and feel the teacher's genuine interest. Make the conference a time where people talk together about things that matter to them.

Ideas and Implications for Classroom Practice

1. Hold conferences mostly on an informal basis at the student's desk, or wherever the writing is occurring, when the purpose is studying on-stage writing. On the other hand, when the purpose is studying or learning more about off-stage writing (or to help children with any writing problems), a conference can be prearranged and held by appointment at a writing center or elsewhere. The informal conference should be short, perhaps three to seven minutes, long enough to allow a discussion, but short enough not to interfere too much with the writing. The prearranged conference may go somewhat longer, but keeping it to ten minutes or less will enable the teacher to meet with more students, more often. In general, five minutes will give a teacher time to check writing progress, ask a pertinent question or two, and offer praise for a particularly excellent passage.

2. Use a tape recorder if writing notes seems to get in the way of the conference—or to take too much time from the interview itself.

3. For short conferences and interviews, move around the classroom during writing time with a clipboard and an alphabetized list of students. Jot down notes beside the names of students observed or interviewed so that a record is readily available, showing which students have and have not been checked. This practice will help ensure that no one is ignored, that all get a share of attention.

4. On occasion, stay at a table in the writers' corner of the classroom, observing, yet available for children to approach with questions or for children to initiate conferences.

5. Use information gained from observing and interviewing to direct use of teacher time more effectively. Learn where children in the class are needing the most help: ideas, structure and form, supporting skills, or whatever, and direct efforts accordingly. Learn where individual students are needing help: sustaining effort, organizing, making effective transitions, etc., and give help as needed. Observe what interests, excites, and aids students in their writing, and capitalize on this knowledge in setting the stage for writing. Observe what thinking time or idea-gathering time is important and help students use notebooks or talk to classmates to refresh memory or stimulate ideas.

6. Ask questions that writers should ask themselves about their writing. Help students learn to ask such questions so that they will learn to critique their own writing by holding individual conferences with themselves (see Sowers 1983).

Extending a Student's Writing Time

The amount of time in a school day is fixed during a given term, and any expansion of time must come with more effective use of time and with helping students see that writing does not *have* to stay within the limits of school time. A major time extender in school is the student journal, mainly because journal keeping cuts across class period boundaries. Students can write in journals at any time during the school day, whenever they have a moment, and they can carry journals home with them for out-of-school writing. Other time extenders are on-going bookmaking projects where writing and other language activities are integrated for effective use of time and an attention to the art of nonfiction writing in the curriculum, so that it, too, is a creative effort.

The Journal in School—and Out

Suggested Activities

1. Students keep personal journals as a place to write primarily for themselves or as a notebook for jotting ideas. Sharing is on a voluntary basis, and the teacher does not read the journals unless invited.

2. Students keep personal journals, as above, but the teacher monitors, at least to see that regular entries are being made. The teacher may simply monitor for entries and not read unless passages are specially

marked, or the teacher may read on a regular basis (all except passages marked "private") and offer encouragement and suggestions. This kind of arrangement requires an atmosphere of mutual trust in the classroom.

3. Students keep writing-journals, where they are expected to develop their writing ideas on an on-going basis. This arrangement brings journal keeping into the curriculum as a language arts requirement, and teachers check regularly and write evaluative comments. The checking usually occurs once a week and many teachers write their comments each time in note form in the margins of the journal pages. Kirsten Kaiser, a master teacher at the Common School, Amherst, Massachusetts, writes her "notes" on notepaper and clips her note to the portion of the journal she has read. In this way, she does not put an outsider's writing on anyone's personal writing, and the students can keep their notes, or not, as they like. They probably *do* like to keep the notes, for Kirsten is very positive in her approach. Specific strengths are pointed out and praised or encouraged, and constructive suggestions or helpful questions are given for trouble spots.

4. Students keep journals on a continuing basis, as above, and the writing is part of the requirement of the language arts program; however, because of other projects or because the students are older and prolific, the teacher does not read everything that is entered. Each week, or each regular checking time, the teacher asks the students to mark what they feel is their best writing of the lot (written since last check), and *that* is what the teacher reads and evaluates. This adds writing practice time for students by not limiting them in any way as to *quantity* and saves time for busy teachers who cannot find time for reading lengthy journals. Teachers simply spend time reading what students choose as their best *quality*.

5. In any of the four arrangements listed above, it is helpful for teachers to set aside a given time each day, or at least two or three times a week, for journal writing and not leave it entirely to odd moments or out-of-school times. A definite period for journal writing, like a sustained, silent writing time for the whole class, establishes a commitment to the journal, primes the pump for an idea flow, and helps make journal writing an on-going activity.

Implementing the Practice

1. The journal habit is a good one to cultivate, for students can keep ideas whenever they occur and later have them to draw upon when there is more writing time, such as in the regular language arts class period. It is also a companionable means of talking to oneself in a creative or expressive way, and an excellent outlet for self-expression. Some teachers

give assignments for journals, but these assignments seem to bring the whole activity out of the personal journal category and into a series of language arts or writing assignments, no longer a place to jot personal writing, notes, or ideas, but a notebook for subjects imposed from outside the writer.

2. The personal journal is just that—*personal*, and to build the feeling of ownership and uniqueness, teachers often encourage special decorations and titles for the notebooks used as journals.

3. Teachers who are beginning the journal practice in their classrooms will want to show students that they, too, keep journals. This kind of modeling helps in encouraging students to feel that the journal is a valued practice. Another kind of modeling is found in children's literature. Many favorite characters keep journals, including Anastasia of *Anastasia Krupnik* by Lois Lowry (Houghton Mifflin, 1979) and Jenny in *Poor Jenny, Bright As A Penny* by Shirley R. Murphy (Viking, 1974).

4. If grading is thought necessary, a teacher can grade on the basis of whether or not the journal is kept faithfully, and not on the basis of journal content, to keep from   violating the personal nature of the material.

5. To give journal writing status, a teacher can point out that many authors keep journals. Author Patricia Lee Gauch (1983) says that a journal is a gift one gives to oneself.

6. A journal is one of the best ways to keep writing flowing and a good way for teachers and students to get an overview of longitudinal progress.

7. Teacher response to journals can be the pivotal point in determining the success or failure of the journal as a part of the language arts program. How the teacher receives the writing in the journal or treats the personal nature of the journal is crucial.

Teacher Response to Student Journals

1. Establish trust. Give student writers the respect that is due any author. Respect privacy and "publish" student writing only with permission.

2. Work with parents to develop the same kind of trust between student and parent as exists between student and teacher.

3. Use a positive approach. Be sure that all comments, oral and written, are constructive, encouraging, and helpful.

4. If grades for writing are required, consider grading a final paper that might emerge from a journal idea, rather than grading journal entries.

5. View longitudinal progress of student writers by means of journal entries written over a period of time. Help students appreciate their own growth as they look at entries made during a school term.

The Journal as Springboard to Other Writing

1. Show students that journals are good for "capturing ideas." Many established authors use journals to capture ideas, which they later develop into longer pieces of writing, from poems to novels. Students can also develop the practice of jotting ideas in journals for later reference or expansion.

2. Use journals as a means of "discovery." Since writing is a way of learning and of discovering personal meaning, the journal provides an important place for discovery because it permits exploration. One can write without constraint in a journal. It is, in fact, a place to brainstorm on paper. Later, when the writer looks over the brainstorming, an idea may present itself for polishing, for developing into something to share with others.

3. Writing in journals keeps a writer in "practice." The more a student writes, it is likely the more at ease he or she will feel in writing. Journal writing builds confidence for other kinds of writing.

4. Teachers sometimes need to stimulate journal writing itself. Provocative questions can let students have some options and help with idea gathering, stimulating rather than stifling personal writing. Possible questions for teachers to suggest that children ask themselves are as follows:

> For what reasons am I glad to be alive today?
>
> What did I see that was interesting on the way to school today?
>
> What is the most interesting place in our school?
>
> What is the most unusual part of our community?
>
> If I could travel anywhere I wanted, where would I go and why?
>
> What do I want to know more about, and what are some questions that I have about it?
>
> What is happening around me at this very moment: what all can I describe if I observe carefully?
>
> What person would I like most to be like? What characteristics do I admire in that person?
>
> What makes me feel ill at ease or uncomfortable? What can I do to help myself feel better about it?
>
> How do I feel about my journal today?

An Ongoing Bookmaking Project

Time spent on the various language arts does not have to be additive. When ways to interrelate the arts are used, many of the language arts can be experienced in one period. Building a language arts curriculum around a long-term bookmaking project is a way to put writing at the center of the program and to ensure that there is substantial writing time.

Phyllis DeMass, the teacher who worked with Mike, Jim, and Elizabeth (see the Theory and Research section of this book), has developed a language arts program around bookmaking. This program was developed during the years Phyllis taught at the McGuffey Laboratory School, Miami University, Oxford, Ohio.

I. General Objectives

   A. Provide each child with multiple opportunities for the practical use of language skills: reading, written expression, oral language, handwriting, spelling, etc.

   B. Provide each child with an opportunity to complete, in an interesting, worthwhile, attractive way, a project that is uniquely his or hers and in which the child can take pride.

   C. Provide a focal point for
     1. relating language and art,
     2. meaningful sharing (children love to read these books to other students: peers, lower-grade students, etc.),
     3. identifying needed skills and developing checklists with children, and
     4. creating additional enthusiasm for reading and writing.

   D. There are *many* specific objectives possible which, as in teaching units, would be related directly to the particular class and each student.

II. Materials Needed (This is enough to get the basic job done; *many* variations are possible.)

   Supply of easy picture books for children to browse through, read, analyze, etc.

   Writing paper, pencils

   Rulers

   Compasses, or some other sharp-pointed object for punching holes for stitching

   Newsprint, drawing paper, or some other suitable unlined paper at least 12″ × 18″ for making the "dummy" copy

   Heavy-weight, white art paper, at least 12″ × 18″, heavy enough so that felt lettering pencils can be used on both sides without soaking through paper

   Fine-pointed black felt markers for final lettering

   Assortment of colored map or drawing pencils, crayons, water colors, various kinds of colored paper, etc., for illustrations

Lightweight poster board or cardboard for covers

Lightweight string or twine for stitching

Needles with eyes large enough for the twine

Glue or paste

Cloth, burlap, colored paper, contact paper or whatever for covering the cardboard cover (or cardboard covers can be left plain)

III. Production Steps

Related Suggestions

A. Child writes a story that he or she wants to "finish" into book form. For reluctant writers: No "correctness" pressure; encourage child to just tell the story. Last resort: let the child paraphrase a favorite story, using the actual story book as a model; encourage child to make as many changes as possible, and to move away from this kind of dependence as soon as he or she is able.

Read to children and encourage them to read many easy picture books. Look at the Caldecott Award books. Let children tape record stories and show pictures as tape is played to class. Use story records or films, if available. Discuss obvious characteristics of easy picture books: simple plots, interesting illustrations, etc. (It helps at this stage to point out form characteristics of easy picture books: margins, letter and line spacing, overall layout. Some children have a difficult time with these features in their own books.)

B. Each child proofreads the finished story with the teacher. This needs to be done with the teacher, in a one-to-one situation, no matter how good the story or the child is.

Provide differing amounts of proofreading help for different children. Provide as much help as the children need to move on from this point, even if, in some cases, it means making some corrections for them.

This is the one critical point at which the whole project can really bog down, since the teacher is directly needed with all children. At most other stages, children can teach or help each other.

Keep needed skill teaching related to, but separate from, periods of time devoted to work on the book project itself (except for on-the-spot explanations when proofreading).

Instead of starting the whole class on the bookmaking project at once, start just one group at a time (one reading

Develop class or individual checklists of skills learned, skills that need improvement, work habits that are desirable, etc. These are excel-

group works very well). Get the group past this first proof-reading job before starting the next group. Start with the "slowest" group. They will need more detailed help, more motivation, more time, more everything! (The only exception is when the teacher thinks another group's work would spark interest for reluctant writers.)

C. Child makes a second copy of story (regular paper) incorporating all changes and corrections.

Teacher rechecks this copy for any mistakes that have slipped through (does not necessarily need to be done with child—great for the teacher's homework!).

D. Child makes "dummy" (practice) copy of book:
  1. decides on desired size,
  2. folds pages of paper and lays pages, one inside the other, and
  3. determines margins, spacing for lines, size of lettering, location of illustrations.

E. Teacher checks finished "dummy" with child, helps with counting number of pages needed in final book.

F. Child sizes and folds good paper for book, being sure to

lent as a basis for evaluating each child's work as the project proceeds and at the end.

Usually help is needed with using rulers for measuring straight lines, etc.; manuscript writing; identifying the beginning format of a book—half-title page, full title page, copyright, dedication, how pages are numbered, and so on. A picture book can be used as a model for format.

Some whole-class or whole-group instruction on measuring, manuscript writing, and format cuts down on the amount of individual help required during work periods.

allow enough pages for everything that he or she wants in the book. Child draws guide lines for printing and makes pencil copy of story, leaving room for illustrations.

G. Teacher does one more quick proofreading job, if needed. Child goes over words with fine felt-tip marker.

H. Child adds illustrations. These can be drawn directly in book, or can be finished on other paper and pasted in book.

Encourage and present different ways of illustrating. Some children can simply cut pictures from magazines and paste them in book.

I. Cardboard is measured and cut for the cover, slightly larger than the pages. Allow a quarter inch for the spine of the book. Score the cardboard (make a line with a sharp point where the fold is to go), and it will fold evenly.

Children who have progressed beyond this point with their own books can teach and help other children.

J. Clip the pages on the cover as firmly as possible. Using a ruler and pencil, place marks on the center fold for the stitching holes, not closer than ¼". Leave margins of ½" at the top and bottom if cover is to be covered with other material.

K. Using a sharp object (compass point), punch holes through pages and cardboard at points marked.

If the project is introduced and taught early enough in the year so that children can learn to independently handle mechanics of construction, and if needed materials can be made available in the room, some children will work at continuing projects (finishing one book and beginning another). This is an excellent work activity for spare time.

L. Using twine and needle, stitch pages into cover.

M. Measure and cut burlap, cloth, or other covering material, if a cover for the cardboard is desired, making it large enough to bend over the edges. Spot glue. Cut paper (slightly smaller than cover) to paste inside front and back covers to hide raw edges of material.

N. Put title on and decorate front of book. Use felt, scraps of material, marking pens, yarn, cut-out letters, etc.

Interrelating Writing with All the Language Arts

A bookmaking project begins with oral discussion, reading aloud, listening, critical evaluation of form and content of various picture books, gathering ideas for possible stories to develop, and drafting. The writing (and rewriting) of the stories for the books involves sharpening composition skills and using appropriate supporting skills of spelling, punctuation, usage conventions, etc. The rewriting grows out of critical rereading. Conferences, questions, advice, and other oral activity continue. At all stages of the work, the language arts are integrated in a purposeful project. Students learn skills as they apply them, in a natural and integrated way.

Other ways to interrelate writing with all the language arts include oral and written response to books, writing to learn about favorite authors (letters to the authors themselves and to publishers), and creating a class anthology of stories or a class newspaper.

Guidelines for interrelating the language arts through a class project are as follows:

Have a purpose or a central focus for any project; make sure that children share a commitment to the project's purpose.

Help children see relationships in the language arts and how interrelating can aid learning.

Build on the natural relationships (i.e., listening and speaking; writing and reading). Don't force relationships or overdo.

Set the stage for "integration" projects, such as the bookmaking project, but let children participate in the planning.

Let children be part of the ongoing evaluation of a project. (What is going well? What can we do better?)

Give dignity to the outcomes or products of any project. Recognize accomplishments; help children feel that their efforts are worthwhile. Make class projects "special."

Integrating the Writing Project with Other Subject Areas

The bookmaking focus can be extended to other subject areas. For example, it can be a "utopia" project involving almost all the areas of the curriculum. An excellent reference for this kind of project is Richard Murphy's *Imaginary Worlds* (1974). In a "Create Your Own Utopia" project, students do just that: create a world of their choosing. They can make it any way they like, as realistic or fantastic as they wish. To get started, students should become familiar with or review some other-world stories, such as C. S. Lewis's *The Lion, the Witch, and the Wardrobe* (Macmillan, 1951) about Narnia or Lloyd Alexander's *The Book of Three* (Holt, Rinehart and Winston, 1964) about Prydain.

Students may read several other-world stories and also listen to excerpts read by their teacher. Then they can begin to create their own utopias, first by describing, then by mapping, and sometimes by illustrating through drawing or painting. Writing the description or setting begins in the language arts, but mapping takes students into social studies and drawing takes them into art. Next students tell the story of how they travel to their utopias, whether through a secret door, by space travel, or however.

The directions to take are almost unlimited, as students decide everything from climate to government of their domains. Questions and suggestions that students might consider are as follows:

What does it look like? Describe it. Draw a map of it.

How did you get there?

Are there schools? What are they like?

What kind of government will you have?

Are there any known problems or enemies? What can you do about them?

What kinds of leisure-time activities are there?

Will there be careers in utopia? What are the opportunities?

These questions and suggestions show how the utopia project can begin to spread throughout the curriculum as students write books about their utopias. Figure 1 illustrates how the writing about utopias can relate and interrelate with other subject areas. It provides a network of possibilities, all branching out from a focus on creating other worlds, or worlds of writers' imaginations.

In some areas of the curriculum, such as social studies, science, or health, students will want to draw upon some nonfiction accounts of the phenomena of our own world to get ideas for their creations. In this way, the utopia project can provide a springboard for finding out more about our own real world.

Important Nonfiction Writing

Reporting In-school and Out-of-school Interviews as a Way of Writing and Knowing

Interviews are an important way of learning and can provide a valuable extension of educational resources, as students learn from interviewing

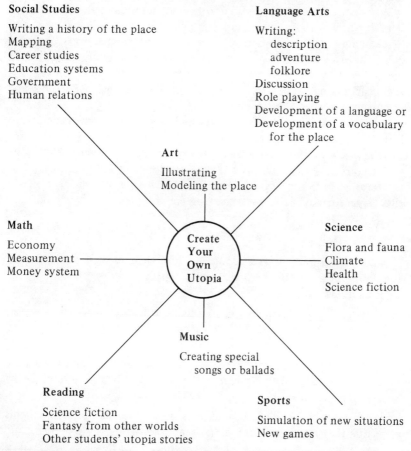

Social Studies

Writing a history of the place
Mapping
Career studies
Education systems
Government
Human relations

Language Arts

Writing:
    description
    adventure
    folklore
Discussion
Role playing
Development of a language or
Development of a vocabulary
    for the place

Art

Illustrating
Modeling the place

Math

Economy
Measurement
Money system

Create Your Own Utopia

Science

Flora and fauna
Climate
Health
Science fiction

Music

Creating special
    songs or ballads

Reading

Science fiction
Fantasy from other worlds
Other students' utopia stories

Sports

Simulation of new situations
New games

Figure 1. A Network of Suggestions for Relating the Utopia Project to Different Areas of the Curriculum.

knowledgeable people. Students can also learn more about themselves and each other through interviews. Writing skills involved include writing questions to take to the interview, note taking during the interview, and writing up the interview afterwards.

1. Let students interview each other, perhaps as a way of getting better acquainted at the beginning of a school year. Video tape (or audio tape) the interviews and let students watch and/or listen to their own performance afterwards. Help students become more at ease with the interview technique. The audience can use these sessions to practice note taking of interesting points and supporting details. Have students take turns until everyone has a chance at every role: interviewer, subject of the interview, observer, and note taker.

2. Use the interview technique to help students campaign for class or school offices. Let student volunteers interview all candidates who wish to campaign in this way. Give volunteers an opportunity to prepare questions prior to assuming the role of interviewer. Encourage students in the audience to take notes to help them remember the high points about each candidate. Student reporters can write accounts of candidates' statements for class or school newspaper.

3. Branch out into the community and use the interview technique to learn more about current class interests or course subject matter. If the class is studying about Australia, for example, arrange for an interview with a community resident who has traveled there recently, or if the class is interested in sports, arrange for an interview with a local sports celebrity. General guidelines for interviewing are as follows:

> Divide the class into committees for interviews in which they are interested.

> Let students call, ask permission for the interview, and make an appointment. (In the lower grades, arrange for the subject of the interview to come to the school.)

> Help students learn to prepare questions for the interview that provide for the courtesies of interviewing, including using the interview time well.

> Provide for an escort (parent or aide) for the interview committee and get necessary permissions if the interview is to take place off school grounds.

> Let students take small note pads where they can jot down items that they want to remember. (A tape recorder can also be used.)

> Encourage students to write an interview report as soon as possible, while everything is fresh in their minds.

> Allow students to share their reports orally or develop a class file of

interview reports for others to read. Some reports may be included in a school or class newspaper.

As the above suggestions show, interviewing is one more way to take writing experience beyond the language arts class time and into other areas.

Gathering Material for and Writing the Modern Newscast

The newscast is a means for combining writing in a specialized form with social studies. It also provides for much practice with all of the language arts: listening, speaking, reading, and writing. Note taking and script writing are forms of writing important for students to know.

1. Have students watch newscasts on television, then discuss at school, and outline main parts and features.

2. Encourage students to discuss current news events as they hear about them or read about them in newspapers.

3. Divide the class into groups to create their own newscasts and let each group sign up for a time to present their newscast to the class. (One group per week allows the teacher and class to incorporate the newscast in a unit on current events.)

4. Ask each group to appoint an "anchor person" to lead the group's preparations and serve as leader in the newscast.

5. As the time approaches for a group's presentation, review the steps: listen to the latest television newscasts, read news accounts in papers and magazines, take notes, and create scripts. (During the weeks of others' presentations, students will learn from critiquing others' work.)

6. At the appointed time for a presentation, arrange for students to sit at a table in front of the class and "give their show." As in television newscasts, the anchor person presides and moves things along, while various members of the group share the parts they have been responsible for preparing: local news, national news, international news, sports, weather, etc.

7. Guide students' experience in reading from notes, looking up at the audience, and keeping up a smooth-running report or commentary.

8. Use video tape, if available, or audio tape, to record the newscasts for later replaying, reviewing, and critiquing.

9. Write to a local radio or television station for examples of scripts to learn more about this kind of writing.

Multi-source Research Projects

Gathering information from more than one source to include in a report takes special skills in note taking, abstracting main ideas (interesting, pertinent, whatever one is looking for), and organizing. Young children can begin by using at least two sources. For example, when writing about a well-known person, the child can consult an encyclopedia account and a biography, taking selected high points from each and organizing them into a report that he or she finds interesting. This is yet another kind of project that takes writing across curricular boundaries, since reports can be a useful way to share information in many subject areas.

1. Bring into class at least two accounts of the same topic and share both. Have students tell the main points (or most interesting) in each account. List main points on the chalkboard. Let children help organize the main points or ideas into one cohesive report. Show how to give credit to the sources.

2. When students have "walked through" the procedure as a class, encourage them to try writing their own reports on current class subjects or on topics of their own choosing.

3. Develop a research project that involves using several sources with older students. This kind of project can be a focal point for relating writing and the other language arts, just as a fiction project can be. Specific writing skills to be developed include finding references or sources, note taking, summarizing, retelling in one's own words, organizing, drafting, rewriting, and editing.

4. Reserve a class bulletin board for an information exchange. Students can post their topics so that others can share clippings or references that they come across in doing their own research.

Writing About Writing

A good way to find out more about writing is to write about it. Students explore their feelings about writing and learn more about these feelings as they *write about writing,* just as they learn more about any topic through writing about it. Also, for the child who has a block or can't think of any ideas, writing about writing can give something to write about and sometimes leads into ideas for further writing. Finally, students' written comments on writing provide another means of observation for the teacher. When students write about their pleasures and frustrations with writing, it can be enlightening to teachers. Teachers can learn a lot about *time for writing* from comments such as these from the McGuffey Laboratory School, Miami University, Oxford, Ohio (spring 1983).

> Usually I like writing. I like it more if I can write what I want to and usually I don't write as well when I'm assigned something.
>
>   Peter (Intermediate Grades)
>
> I don't like writing because it's boring, especially when I don't have any ideas.
>
>   Heather (Intermediate Grades)

I usually enjoy writing creatively. . . . Sometimes, however, I have trouble being creative enough. I often sit for an hour with a pencil in hand and not write a word.

Eric (Eighth Grade)

Writing is thinking of something to write.
Writing is searching all over your mind,
Scrounging, deciding, and finally putting your
Thoughts on a blank piece of paper, and
making it beautiful with just some
little words put together.

Leora (Eighth Grade)

Sources Cited

Beeker, Ruth Ann. *The Effects of Oral Planning on Fifth Grade Composition.* North Texas State University: University Microfilms, 1970.

Birnbaum, June Cannell. "The Reading and Composing Behavior of Selected Fourth- and Seventh-Grade Students." *Research in the Teaching of English* 16 (October, 1982): 241–260. (ERIC No. EJ 268 133).

Dyson, Anne Haas, and Celia Genishi. "'Whatta Ya Tryin' to Write?': Writing as an Interactive Process." *Language Arts* 59 (February, 1982): 126–132. (ERIC No. EJ 257 840).

Eldridge, Mabel E. "Anecdotes about American Authors." In *New Directions in Children's Literature*, edited by Eileen Tway. Report on the Proceedings of the Fifth Annual Conference on Children's Literature, Miami University, Oxford, Ohio, 1976.

Emig, Janet A. *The Composing Process of Twelfth Graders.* Urbana, Ill.: National Council of Teachers of English, 1971.

Emig, Janet A. "Writing as a Mode of Learning." In *The Writing Teacher's Sourcebook*, edited by Gary Tate and Edward P. J. Corbett. New York: Oxford University Press, 1981.

Gauch, Patricia Lee. "On Journals." Miami University Writing Workshop, July, 1983.

Graves, Donald H. "Children's Writing: Research Directions and Hypotheses Based upon an Examination of Writing Processes of Seven-year-old Children." Ed.D. diss., State University of New York at Buffalo, 1973. (ERIC Document Reproduction Service No. ED 095 586).

Graves. Donald H. Interview. Durham, New Hampshire, May 26, 1983.

Graves, Donald H. Research report given at the International Reading Association Annual Convention. Chicago, Ill., April 29, 1982.

Graves, Donald H. "The Child, the Writing Process, and the Role of the Professional." In *The Writing Process of Students*, edited by Walter T. Petty and Patrick J. Finn. Buffalo, N.Y.: State University of New York at Buffalo, 1975.

Henry, George H. "Introduction." *English Education* 12 (October, 1980): 4.

Johnson, Wendell. "You Can't Write Writing." In *The Use and Misuse of Language*, edited by S. I. Hayakawa. Greenwich, Conn.: Fawcett, 1962.

Lopate, Phillip. "Helping Young Children Start to Write." In *Research on Composing: Points of Departure*, edited by Charles R. Cooper and Lee Odell, Urbana, Ill.: National Council of Teachers of English, 1978, p. 141.

Murphy, Richard. *Imaginary Worlds.* New York: Teachers and Writers Collaborative, 1974.

Murray, Donald M. "Internal Revision: A Process of Discovery." In *Research on Composing: Points of Departure*, edited by Charles R. Cooper and Lee Odell. Urbana, Ill.: National Council of Teachers of English, 1978, p. 100.

Murray, Donald M. "Write Before Writing." In *The Writing Teacher's Sourcebook*, edited by Gary Tate and Edward P. J. Corbett. New York: Oxford University Press, 1981, p. 171.

Smith, Frank. *Writing and the Writer*. New York: Holt, Rinehart, and Winston, 1982, p. 106.

Sowers, Susan. "Reflect, Expand, Select: Three Responses in the Writing Conference." In *Understanding Writing*, edited by Thomas Newkirk and Nancie Atwell. Chelmsford, Mass.: The Northeast Regional Exchange, Inc., 1982, p. 89.